D0684835

Aren't You Glad You're Old?

A Humorous Look at Life in Older Years

Marie Albertson

AREN'T YOU GLAD YOU'RE OLD?
A HUMOROUS LOOK AT LIFE IN OLDER YEARS

iUniverse books may be ordered through booksellers or by contacting:

iUniverse
1663 Liberty Drive
Bloomington, IN 47403
www.iuniverse.com
844-349-9409

Because of the dynamic nature of the Internet, any web addresses or links contained in this book may have changed since publication and may no longer be valid. The views expressed in this work are solely those of the author and do not necessarily reflect the views of the publisher, and the publisher hereby disclaims any responsibility for them.

Any people depicted in stock imagery provided by Getty Images are models, and such images are being used for illustrative purposes only. Certain stock imagery © Getty Images.

ISBN: 978-1-6632-1334-1 (sc)
ISBN: 978-1-6632-1333-4 (e)

Library of Congress Control Number: 2021902664

Print information available on the last page.

iUniverse rev. date: 02/16/2021

To Helen for giving me a great idea for a book. To Jonna for being my photographer (front and back cover) and grandkids for encouragement and motivation. Love you all.

INTRODUCTION

I am an eighty-plus-year-old retired librarian. I say "retired" with reluctance. I consider myself still employable; however, I haven't found the right employer who wants to hire an old librarian. I reinvented myself at age sixty-three when I unloaded a five-bedroom house in a small town where I had lived for forty years where my late husband and I had raised four children and then packed up my little Ford and moved to Indianapolis.

I had quit my job in the local library and headed south with the thought of easily finding a new job (another adventure in the making). If I had any reluctance, it dissipated when I looked in my back seat, completely covered with stuff I hadn't put in storage, and realized I was making the right move. It was then I came to believe in angels. I felt the presence of angelic figures pushing me on to my first solo adventure. I just knew my angels were with me, so onward I went.

After arriving in Indy and having a few disastrous job interviews, I was lucky enough to land a job at the Indiana State Library (another thing influenced by my angels, I am sure). I worked at the State Library in the Library Development Office for seven years. My position required me to work with institutional libraries around the state. I worked with and visited mental health facilities, correctional institutions, and special health facilities, such as the Indiana Blind School and the School for the Deaf.

I enjoyed the position very much, but at age seventy

I decided to retire. I was thinking seriously of moving to Arizona and sitting in the sun; however, at age sixty-five, I was introduced to a grandson I didn't know too well. Within the next few weeks, I was lucky enough to have him as a permanent roommate, another adventure. We have had our challenges, but I think we maneuvered through life's vagaries quite well.

At that point, I felt the need to work on another degree and line of work. So I enrolled at a local community college. Incidentally, I found a college where retired persons over sixty-five could attend classes for free. If you are interested in working on another line of work, check in your vicinity to find colleges that offer free or reduced-cost classes to retired people. It is worth the pursuit. After three years of attending classes part-time, I earned an associate's degree in human services (counseling).

With a new set of knowledge, I had a desire to work with older women, especially those in my age group who really had not accomplished in life what they really had wanted to. After writing two books, *Old Librarians Never Die, They Jump Out of Airplanes* and *Fifty Shades of Grey Humor*, I felt I was in a position to confidently speak before women's groups to encourage and motivate them to be more adventurous.

My love of the outdoors emerged, and I became interested in kayaking. After completing the classes, I signed up with an outdoor travel company to take a trip to the Colorado River to kayak in Arizona. Since then, I have kayaked in many spots in the Southwest and rivers in Alaska, the Coral Sea in Australia, the Galapagos Island, San Juan Islands, and Copenhagen. If you haven't had the pleasure of visiting rivers and waterways in the United States and around the world, put that on your to-do list. You can't imagine the beauty of the waters until you are actually on them.

I encourage you to be more adventurous and not be afraid to step out of your safety zone. If you get anything from reading my book, step up and take that leap of faith. With that one step or leap, you will be surprised where it can take you. Happy adventuring.

KAYAKING IN SAN JUAN ISLANDS

ANTIQUES ROADSHOW

Antiques Roadshow came to town! When I heard about it, I quickly dialed the phone number to get a ticket to attend. I surely had enough old items around the house to take and impress the judges. I thought, *May be old but not gold.* I told myself, *Let's give it a shot. I may end up as one of the few attendees to be interviewed on TV.*

While waiting for someone to answer the phone, I dreamed about the judge extolling the wonderful painting I had just purchased at a yard sale a week ago for one dollar. After talking endlessly about my good eye to acquire such a lovely antique, she finally announced the value: $75,000. Oh my! What should I do: faint like the man with a surprisingly valuable old watch still in the original box or act like the Brits and be casual about my lucky find?

The *Roadshow* representative came on the line. I requested a ticket, certain it would be my ticket to early retirement. Unfortunately all the tickets for the Indianapolis show were gone. But she needed workers and asked if I would I be willing to work on the show. Well, that might be the only chance to come close to the show's proceedings. Plus, I could bring one article of mine to be appraised.

I was trained one afternoon. The next day I would become an assistant to a judge on the national show. I did not know what was involved with being a judge's assistant, but I soon found out. The day of the show started early for the assistants.

I had to be at the convention center by 7:00 a.m. Little did I know that I would be at the center until 7:00 p.m. It was a long day.

Luckily I was assigned to assist the painting judge. I had seen her on TV enough to practically call her a friend. She was congenial, and I noticed she was especially nice to the people who brought what they considered a valuable painting. No matter how invaluable it turned out to be, the judge was extremely considerate and kind.

I learned a lot about *Antiques Roadshow* by asking questions of anyone I could ask. We had thirty minutes for lunch. Yes, the lunches were set up for assistants and judges. I sat down with a woman who happened to be a doll judge from Iowa. She had been a judge at many of the shows. She revealed that the rate of finding a doll of great value was about one per show. She also said the judges were not paid and covered their own expenses. The acclaim from the show was their recompense.

The number of people who want to be on the show is phenomenal. To manage such a large amount of people takes unparcelled organization. Once you acquire your ticket, you are assigned a time to be at the show. And you had better be there at your allotted time span or you do not get in. It seems rather strict, but it does eliminate total mass confusion if everyone shows up at the same time.

I enjoyed the day and as a reward was given a blue, short-sleeved shirt with the yellow *AR* logo emblazoned on the left corner. It was a long day of standing and corralling each set of five-person attendees in my line. And no, my painting did not add much to my retirement fund; however, it did turn into another adventure in my life.

I still religiously watch the show and know that I have met or at least been close to many of the judges, even the guy with the wild suits. Incidentally, the producers can realize their TV shows from each city they visit.

"It may be old but still not gold" stands the test of time. Even if your Aunt Molly's silver platter is not as valuable as members of the family proclaim, it would be a fun day for you. As many of the interviewed attendees say at the end of the show, "We had a great time."

Recommended reading: *Kovels' Antiques & Collectibles Price List* by Ralph M. Kovel.

GET A GRIP

I have come to grips that my grip is not what it used to be. Have you found yourself dropping more things than you used to? Cups, keys, and silverware suddenly seem to be more slippery than they were. Or is it our grip or grasp? The power or ability to grasp seems to be slipping away as we age.

I was having lunch with an older friend. When she rose from her chair, she dropped something. She was complaining about bending over to pick up the dropped object. She mumbled, "I drop everything."

I had been experiencing the same dropping problem. Along with the dropping came the problem of retrieving what I had dropped. By the way, how many bend-overs do we have in life? Every time I am bent in half, that question does come to mind. Yes, how many bend-overs do we have in life before we are finally laid out horizontally?

Getting back to dropping, the reason I was dropping so much was that my grip was so weak. The problem wasn't in the dropping; it was in the gripping. After doing some research, I learned as we grow older, some things do loosen up, including our grip.

Grip strengthening is easier and more accessible than other forms of training. Much of it can be done sitting down, lying down, or even while waiting for a red light to change. Invest in a cheap little hand grip or a squeeze ball to grip repeatedly.

What you want to do is strengthen the muscles in your hands. A few recommended exercises include the following:

- Improve grip with hand-strengthening equipment like stress balls, therapy putty, or hand exercisers.
- Do some finger walking and opening-closing exercises to improve flexibility and dexterity.
- Practice wringing out a washcloth to improve your wrist and forearm strength.

Try these exercises daily to keep your hands and wrists strong and nimble. If you are consistent, you will start to see all the benefits that come with grip training. Watch out when you offer a handshake. You may surprise your friend and yourself with your newfound grip strength. If your friend drops to the floor, you have probably done enough grip strengthening.

Recommended reading: *Mystery of Hand Strength* by John Brookfield.

FITBIT

If I see one more person with a Fitbit on one more wrist and not mine, I am going to throw up. And what really gets me is the proud look on the owner's face, as though she is so much more athletically attuned than I am. I sometimes do fifty jumping jacks a day as Dr. Oz prescribed, even though the jacks are a little modified. Maybe jumping "jills" may describe them a little better. No arm raises are involved.

What I think the world needs is Sitbit. If you feel yourself sitting too long watching TV, what you need is a Sitbit. Let's face it. We are all guilty of this. It is just too easy to turn on TV and become quickly engrossed in some mindless family drama that we could easily do without. Anyway, this little Sitbit comes with its own sticky side and a little timer, say one hour or two at most. When you are most vulnerable to find yourself in front of the TV, stick it in your buttocks. Be sure to set the timer. And when the time is up, you get repeated pokes in the old buttocks until you get up and do something useful.

As a librarian, I am more attracted to a Litbit. This encourages you to read more books. Litbit will remind you to read more books and record the names of the books. Litbit attaches to your wrist, and within a minute, you could tap it and impress your friends on your choice of literary works.

How about a Witbit. We all need more humor in our lives, especially now. A little or a lot of wittiness is a good idea.

According to "50 Life Secrets and Tips," one should smile more often.

> Whenever you get a grin on your face, your brain is releasing serotonin, the happy hormone. Smiling is the natural way to force yourself to be happy. It is a very powerful tool that is utilized less and less as we grow older and need happiness more than ever. Just remember that while happiness leads to smiles, smiles also lead to happiness.

If a smile can do that much for you, just think what a good laugh, a hearty guffaw, can do for you. Remember this number one rule: you need to laugh at least six times a day. Laughing is great medicine and a good exercise for your facial muscles.

Writbit denotes a writing nudge. In these trying times, one should write every day. Take pen to paper, notebook, or napkin and put down your thoughts. Write and describe how you are feeling about current events. We are living in an unusual time. History buffs will have a field day writing about this era. You will look back at this time in ten years or so and be surprised at how you maneuvered through these trying times. Become your own historian. Your grandchildren or great-grandchildren will be interested in knowing what Grandma and/or Granddad were doing and thinking during this pandemic.

Pitbit reminds you to pitch something (not a fit). Do something athletic other than running. Pick up any-sized ball and then bounce it, throw it, or pitch it. Find someone to play catch with. Or by yourself, just throw it up in the air and catch It. It's good exercise for eye/hand coordination. Plus, if you drop it a lot, retrieving the ball is good exercise.

Nitbit is not to be confused with nitwit. It reminds you to stay away from the nitwits who are nitpickers, those always negative people. Don't allow yourself to fall into that trap of negativity. Distance yourself from the nitpickers. If you find yourself thinking negative thoughts, jump up and down. Do something physical or scream. Do whatever it takes to stay positive. Everyone around you will appreciate it, and you will feel better for it.

Recommended reading: *Strength Training for Seniors: How to Rewind Your Biological Clock* by Michael Fekete.

SEEING FAITH

I bounded up the stone steps of the neighborhood church on a glorious sunny weekday, one of my favorite times for a solitary commune with God. I pushed open the wooden door and walked into the interior of the church, and a vast emptiness enveloped me. My eyes strained through the blackness crowding the church. My first thought was, *Why stay? It may be dangerous to be alone in this unlighted area, even in a church.* Looking toward the altar, nothing was discernible, just murky darkness.

I sat down in the last pew with just enough light to read the large print in a black prayer book. After reading a few minutes, I glanced up. Surprisingly, objects were beginning to appear. They were still faint, but the wood-grained pews came into view. Light shifted through the haze; tiny bits of dust floated in the air. Objects, totally unseeable at first, began to take shape and become clear. I could now see the huge marble crucifix hanging behind the altar. Colored light rays streaked through the stained-glass windows. Why did I ever doubt? Some may say my eyes adjusted to the darkness. I prefer to think my faith adjusted to time.

I wondered why I ever thought of leaving the church before I could see, before I could distinguish the interior of this beautiful little church. I suddenly realized the true meaning of faith. It involves patience and time. The valleys of faith contain days, sometimes years, of not seeing clearly.

Many times in my life, I have lived with fear and impatience. I wanted to give up, run away, or leave early.

Faith is outlasting the doubts of murky darkness until a time of seeing or revelation comes. With enough faith, darkness will disappear, fear will dissipate, and horizons of faithful tranquility will come into view.

Recommended reading: *Bringing the Light and Conversations with God* by Neale Donald Walseh.

TRAVELER

Open your universe. There's a big world out there. While you are still here on this earth and upright, get out and explore your surroundings, near or far. Talk to any traveler, and they will either bore you with all the details or give you the urge to pack your bag and take a trip. Don't let your age or the lack of a traveling companion deter you. More and more singles are signing up for an adventure on the high seas or across the vastness of a land cruise.

I started traveling at age seventy. I first learned how to kayak at age sixty-five. After completing the course, I felt courageous enough to sign on as a kayaker. My first kayaking trip was in Georgia on St. Simon's Island along the Atlantic coast with a group from Road Scholar. At that time, it was called Elderhostel. After a few name changes, it was decided the name of the touring group would be Road Scholar, not denoting any age group and welcoming of any age. I was still working at the Indiana State Library, so I was still on a limited time, ten days or less.

My first kayaking trip turned out to be so enjoyable that I signed up the next year for a river kayaking trip out West. I flew into Phoenix and then jumped on a two-seater plane and bumpily landed in Prescott to get close to my final destination of Chloride, Arizona, an old copper mining town that had lost its copper and slowly died. The population now is two hundred people (maybe). It has one main street, one bar, one post office, and a charming one-room library. The bar must have been there since the rip-roaring days of mining.

When entering the bar, your eyes go immediately to the painting of a naked woman hanging over the bar. Behind the bar was the usual row of whiskey bottles of every make and color. The old bar was battered and bruised and held a history of its own. The dark wooden stools matched the age of the bar. It wasn't difficult to envision many a bar fight between the miners while whooping it up on a Friday night.

After reveling in the long-ago history of this copper town, I met the rest of the kayakers. There were fifteen women, all different ages, roaring and ready for an adventure on the Colorado River. After introductions and exchanging platitudes, we were taken to Lake Mead for our first test. We were assigned a kayak to paddle to the middle of the lake. Once at the lake's center, our fearless leader directed each of us to fall out of the kayak. The next test was to then climb back into the kayak. If we were capable of that maneuver without drowning, we seemingly were river-ready for our weeklong camping trip along the river.

The next day, we drove to the Colorado River with kayaks in tow and deposited right below Hoover Dam. Once I was strapped into my life jacket, I dragged my kayak to the water's edge. Once I got settled into my kayak, I paddled out to see the expanse of the river. I was completely blown away at the beauty of the river. The blue sky overhead, the shimmering sparkling water below, and the green trees along the bank of the river was breathtaking. If you want to see the beauty of any river, get off the highway and go down to the river's edge to enjoy the natural beauty of our country. You will be as thrilled as I was with nature's bounty.

While getting to know my new fellow adventurers, I was entranced to hear of their travels. Many had been to Europe and Asia, even Africa. And I resolved when I got home to travel abroad. That was my goal: travel around the world and visit every continent. Over the next fifteen years, that is exactly what I did.

I have found that making goals is something everyone should do, no matter what age you are. Your goal is to set a goal and then find ways to meet that objective. And believe me, you can do that. You can even travel cheaply. And by traveling, you meet new friends, explore fresh worlds, and realize that most people are alike in everyday living.

We camped along the river at night. Paddling along the Colorado River in the sunshine was a sheer delight. Setting up my tent was a bit of a chore for me the first couple nights, but I conquered it, and by the end of our five-day trip, I became quite adept. We would rise with the sun, have a quick breakfast, and be back on the water as soon as we could. Breakfast consisted mostly of dry cereal, coffee, and orange juice, which our leader set up the night before.

One morning we had a visitor nesting beside the boxes of cereal. A big water snake had decided he'd join us for breakfast and was lying motionless on the setup bar. Our lover-of-wildlife leader carefully scooped up our new friend and put him in a pillowcase. We put him in one of the kayaks. When we reached the next beach area, we turned him loose. And he hurriedly scurried on the sandy area and was quickly out of sight.

I not only made new friends on this trip, but it opened my eyes, my world, and my sense of adventure. Such interesting women I met. One woman from Nevada had been a pilot and was a friend of Mustang Annie, a great admirer of the mustang horses that ranged the desert of the high plains. Annie devoted her life to saving wild horses. One woman's daughter was a noted author of Western novels. Her other daughter was an airline pilot for a national airline. Talk about an interesting family. But these are the people you will meet while traveling outside of your zip code.

Recommended reading: *Fearless Aging: A Journey of Self Discovery, Soul, Work and Empowerment* by Eve Reid.

LEARNING HOW TO FLY A HELICOPTER

TRAVEL

Italian or not, there is a little bit of Christopher Columbus in all of us. Someone gave me a sign that says "We travel not to escape life, but for life not to escape us." Anyone who has traveled extensively will tell you how exciting it is to visit a new land or continent. We humans have been travelers from neanderthal man/woman to now. We like to be on the move.

Visiting a new culture will expand your mind. You may be surprised to find no matter what continent you are on, many of the people who live there are living lives quite like yours. Eating, sleeping, meeting schedules, going to work, and taking care of family are all in anyone's daily agendas.

I was sitting in a small town in Tasmania in a dirt-floor tavern with my group leader, Sunday. (Yes that was his name.) I looked around and realized these people in this bar could be just like my friends at home. At one table sat six local businesswomen dressed in suits—laughing, drinking wine, and enjoying each other's company. Talking business maybe or gossiping, either way, they were enjoying a convivial afternoon with their friends. I learned that people, no matter where they reside, get up in the morning and follow routines just like I do.

If you have an itchy foot, as I do, or want to acquire that itch, do some research on travel or talk to a travel agent in your area. There are many travel clubs in most places. AAA has many trips, both national and international. Overseas

Adventure Travel is one group I have traveled with many times. Grand European Travel (GET) is a group I have been using lately. The trips are shorter, which seems to accommodate my life at this time. AARP is another organization that can help you get you out the door and on the road.

My first trip was to China. I couldn't have picked a destination much farther away except Australia, which I did visit later. Even as a kid, I was interested in the Great Wall. Visiting my small-town library, I could only look at books or magazines about China and dream about how exciting it would be to visit that country so far away. Soon after landing in Beijing, I actually walked on that Great Wall. And yes, it was just as interesting and exciting as I had dreamed it would be.

Don't let a lack of languages dissuade you from travel. You can always find a way to communicate with others in many different ways. You are visiting their land, so you must be respectful. I was sitting at an outside restaurant in Marrakesh, and I looked across the street and saw a rental area for motor scooters. If you have ever been to Marrakesh, you know how many of the citizens use their scooters. It seems everyone—men and women wearing business suits, Muslim women with their burkas flowing in the wind, and workmen with their tools slung over their backs—are zipping in and out of traffic.

I decided to go over to the scooter rental shop and have my picture taken while sitting on one of those high-powered machines. When I got home, I would flash the photo and brag I was driving dangerously through the streets of Marrakesh.

I approached the rental area, and a man dressed in local garb came out of the small house. I, a typical tourist with a camera hung around my neck, asked shyly, "Will you take my picture?"

He was quite friendly and kept smiling, but he obviously could not speak English, and I could not speak any of the three languages of Morocco. I held up my camera and pointed to the shiny black scooter parked in the front of the lot. I looked back at him, and he was shaking his head no. I kept pointing at my chosen scooter, and he kept shaking his head with a solid no.

I hoped I had not said or implied something that hurt his feelings. I did not want to start a war with Morocco. Finally my newfound friend, still smiling, said, "No, red one." He repeated, "Red one." He wanted me to sit on the shiny red scooter, not the shiny black one. Ah, all is well. And that is how you communicate with a new friend, just keep smiling while being persistent. It's another adventure to tell my friends at home. By the way, Moroccans can speak three languages: Arabic, French, and Berber. I vowed I would study a new language when I got home. Shame-faced, I have not.

While in Morocco, our travel group went into the Sahara Desert for a three-night camping trip. On one of our daily rides in the desert, we met a nomad family who all lived in one large tent with their camels and goats staked outside the tent. Three generations lived together: children, parents, and grandparents.

Through an interpreter, one of the grandmothers asked, "Where are your children?"

It was an interesting question. It did show how strong the family ties are to the nomads.

I had the opportunity to take my first camel ride. Actually

it was not a comfortable ride even with the pillows offered by the camel jockeys. I was sore for the week. One night I slept through a sandstorm and didn't even know it. I woke up as the morning sun shone through the tent opening and realized everything, including my bed, was covered with sand.

Morocco and China are two of the countries I had on my travel list. Both countries, as well as the others I have visited, about twenty now, were wonderful that offered once-in-a-lifetime experiences. Don't be afraid to travel. I travel alone until I meet up with the travel group either in Rome, Paris, Sydney, and so forth. You will meet new friends and also have some interesting roommates.

By the way, you can travel inexpensively if you do your research. Many travel companies offer reduced rates at certain times of the year. And many companies are excited to have solo travelers. I have met many female solo adventurers on my trips. Some become lifelong friends through the Internet.

Get your suitcase and start packing.

Recommended reading: *The Bucket List: 1000 Adventures Big and Small*, edited by Kath Strathers.

EXPIRATION DATE

There was a time when I did not pay much attention to the date stamped on items purchased in the grocery store. The words stamped somewhere on the can "Best if used by" and a date would appear. I would grocery-shop, drag bags of canned goods into the kitchen, and store them away in the pantry. Sometimes the cans would be pushed to the back of the pantry and woefully would not be used by their best-if-used-by date, the date on which supposedly the canned goods would no longer be useful, fresh or edible.

Maybe we humans should have a best-if-used-by date or a due date. I know I could have used one. It seems to me I could get a lot more accomplished if I knew when my due date was.

Frankly I never paid much attention to my own due date until lately when I reached my eighth decade. Wouldn't it be nice if we knew our expiration date? Just think how much more we could get done in our time on earth. Maybe at birth, a date should be stamped on our little heads: *Expire on 21MAR2030.*

I don't know about you, but I know for myself I would accomplish more if I knew I only had a certain amount of days/years left. I work much better if I have a schedule with a limited amount of time. I know how much has to be finished by a certain date. Isn't that a due date?

God does us a disservice by not allowing us to know how long we will live. It seems rather harsh, but look at the benefits of knowing your allotted time. There will be no wasting time by idleness and no saving your days. Is there something you always wanted to do but haven't? Do you think, *I'll do it later when I have more money, time, and so on*? And *time* is the key word. We only have so much time, so enjoy yours. Be adventurous.

Recommended reading: *Grand Old Time* by Judy Leigh.

PANDEMIC OF 2020

The modern plague has struck. Coronavirus, COVID-19, or the modern plague has captured the world. Everyone is under siege. The little germ or microorganism that started in China has traveled from Asia to almost every country. And this little germ has cut a wide swath of panic, confusion, and consternation. A complete lack of reliable information coming from our so-called leaders (president and Congress) does not help or calm the nerves of our citizens.

One good thing this little microorganism has done is unite the country in a way I have not seen in a long time. It reminds me of World War II. I was eight years old in fourth grade when I first heard the word *war*. I turned to one of my astute classmates and asked him, "What is war?" He didn't seem to know either except there were guns involved. I soon found out what it meant.

The country soon kicked into a patriotic fever I had never seen before. Now I am seeing a patriotic fever again, a worldwide patriotic fever. Our country and other nations are joining together to fight the one common enemy: coronavirus. We are experiencing rationing for the first time since WWII. You were given a sticker to put in the front window to determine what and how much gas you could purchase in any given week. Sugar was another item that was in short supply. Now it was sinking in; this war stuff was serious. Unfortunately I liked sweet stuff even at that age or especially at the age that has continued into my eighth decade.

We were encouraged to stay home. It's called shelter-in-place. The governor was on TV not only encouraging but almost demanding that we stay put, not to go anywhere unless it was really necessary. Most stores were closed, which didn't bother me too much because I was not much of a shopper anyway. Malls were completely empty. They looked like ghost towns. Schools were closed in March, which amounted to the rest of the school year. Kids were continuing their studies by email, at least for the kids who had working computers at home.

What really changed my way of living was the closing of the local library. The library was my one refuge. And I, a retired librarian, was caught with just one book at home. I usually have at least three or four books going at a time, and here I was with one half-read book on my nightstand. The churches were closed and locked. The services were telecast.

Grocery and hardware stores were considered safe places, but other stores were verboten. Sadly, what I realized was that I was already living a shelter-in-place existence. The grocery store and the hardware store (minus the library) were my life. When this is all over, I have got to develop a new sense of living, to learn a language, volunteer, and expand my sense of purpose.

We were cautioned to not have any social gatherings with friends or relatives with more than ten people attending in fear of spreading the germ.

Traveling was almost wiped out. Hotels closed; the hospitality industry suffered tremendously. Airlines did not have enough passengers to keep flying. I had been used to taking an out-of-the-country trip at least once a year. My wings were clipped. America had the most cases of this virus and sadly the most deaths. If you could find a flight abroad, Europe was off-limits. Europeans did not want Americans entering their countries for fear of bringing and spreading the germ to its citizens.

Social distancing became the rule. If you must go out and mingle with the rest of the citizenry, stay six feet away from other people. They could be carriers. You could be a carrier.

Masks became a new fashion statement. We became a masked society. Everyone had to wear a mask if you wanted to be out in the community. Signs on store windows were posted, "No Mask, No Entrance."

Most professions were changing to stay-at-home positions, adapting easily to working from home rather than going to the office to work. When the school year opened in September, classes were held virtually. Computers became the students' gateway to classes and to teachers working from home.

It was an interesting time in our history. We as older Americans had lived through many historic times in our country, but this was a new one. Most everyone adjusted as well as possible. Getting back to what we called normal was what we all desired. Just as we did in WWII, we can say, "We lived through it."

Recommended reading: *Understanding Coronavirus* by Raul Rabadan.

DOG WALKING MADE EASY

I've seen pictures of dog walkers in New York City, and it looked a little glamorous. Holding a handful of expensive leases for a pack of foo-foo dogs in a big city just had a touch of *Breakfast at Tiffany's on Fifth Avenue.*

So when I saw an ad in a local regional paper for "Dog Walker Wanted," I thought, *What the heck! Why not apply?* Lucky for me after talking to the writer of the ad, she was ready to sign me on. I was invited to go along with a current dog walker. I became a dog walker intern.

Interestingly, I would be working on my 10,000 steps a day, enjoying the fresh air, and caring for lovable little doggies. I have always had pets of my own, including many dogs and cats, rabbits, one chicken that liked to be in the house, a son's snake that escaped from his cage but was found slinking toward the door, and a recalcitrant pony. What's not to like? Plus, I would be getting paid.

I arranged to meet the experienced dog walker (EDW) in the upscale neighborhood at the right hour. The sun was shining brightly with a nice breeze, and trees were in full bloom. What a lovely day for a dog walk! Our first house, or I should say the EDW's first assignment, was a lovely home for which my new friend had a key for the side door. In fact, she had a key ring full of house keys. I asked how many walks she would be doing today, and she said, "Just five."

I was introduced to Sophie, a white long-haired poodle

who apparently had her own room. Also there was a nice couch and a large-screen TV that was on when we walked into her room. Sophie liked to watch TV all day when her owners were at their law or medical offices.

After filling up Sophie's food and water bowls, we were out the door for a good walk around the block. Oh, what a grand day for a walk! After just a few steps, Sophie decided she had to pee, not unusual for a dog. We were two houses down when Sophie decided she had to defecate, to poop, on one of the well-manicured neighbor's front yards. The EDW grabbed a plastic sack out of her well-stocked backpack and stooped over to pick up the poop! Wait a minute! That was part of the job? I was having second thoughts about this. Picking up poop was in the contract?

After four more dog stops and following the procedure of greeting, feeding, walking, and picking up poop, the EDW would grab her phone and click a picture of each of her dogs after finishing all of their duties. The daily photos were then immediately emailed to the dogs' owners, probably to relieve their minds that their beloved pooches were well taken care of one more day.

I remember (in the old days) if you had a dog, you'd open the door, and out he would go. After finishing his toiletries, hopefully in one of the neighbors' yards, you were aware that the neighbor's dog pooped in your yard so it all evened out, especially after a rainstorm. Eventually your dog would come back to the door and whine or claw the screen door until someone let him in the house. Now it seems the dogs are as programmed and helicoptered over as much as the children in the house. Amazing! Oh, for the life of a dog in the twenty-first century.

And have you checked the vet's prices lately? It seems the price of keeping a pet healthy has gone up with the vast number of the newly acquired pets in the country. Maybe I'll buy a fish. There's only the bowl to care for after sprinkling in the fish food confetti. In case of a fish demise, the body's easy to dispose of with one flush and no photographs to prove my guilt.

Recommended reading: *The Business of Dog Walking* by Veronica Boutelle.

NEWSPAPERS

I was raised with a daily newspaper. Reliably every morning on the front porch would be a gallon of milk in a glass bottle and a daily newspaper. Picking up the rolled-up pages, unfolding, and scanning the headlines was exhilarating to me even as a kid. The *Peoria* (IL) *Star* was the name of the paper. The daily newspaper revealed the news of the world. We also subscribed to the small weekly paper that reported the local news. It wasn't much in a town of a thousand people, but I still read it from the front to back page.

I loved the names of the big-city newspapers: *San Francisco Chronicle, Atlanta Journal-Constitution, Chicago Tribune, The New York Times, The Sacramento Bee, The Boston Globe, The Cleveland Plain Dealer,* and *The Arizona Republic.* I was not in a position to pick up one of those papers in its hometown, but maybe I would visit a few of the cities in the future. Just knowing those city newspapers existed and produced the news every day was enough for me to feel important.

Unfortunately my local daily paper now, like most midsized city papers, has decreased in size and news. The Sunday edition can easily be perused in ten to fifteen minutes from the front page to the last. The sports pages are turning into the largest section of the paper. Apparently, athletic scores are more important than world news.

With the advent of social media, Google, smartphones, and so on, we know what is happening in the world while it happens, so why make an effort to search and read about stale news in a local paper? Young people have become accustomed to reading the news immediately. It is disappointing to lose the young readership but understandable.

Interestingly in the late 1990s, newspapers were predicting the closure and uselessness of local libraries. Who needs a library when all the information is at one's fingertips via social media? Fortunately libraries are still here and thriving. (Being a librarian, I am a little biased.) With some regret, I am sorry to say that daily newspapers are losing their patronage.

The newspaper that still has the largest circulation figure is *USA Today* with 2,278,022 papers printed daily. I wonder if this paper had something to do with the decline of the other papers. *USA Today* articles are short, concise, and colorful (the first paper to use color daily) and can be read quickly. The circulation of *The Wall Street Journal* has stayed at 2,062,312, and *The New York Times* comes in third with 1,120,420.

I still subscribe to a daily paper and feel a certain thrill of unwrapping the paper, thumbing through the pages, and enjoying the content of the articles. Don't give up on newspapers. They will survive in some form, I hope.

Recommended reading: *Discovering the News: A Social History of American Newspapers* by Michael Schudson.

SIGNS

Does this world keep adding new signs, or do I just keep finding them? For example, I am at the grocery store on Saturday morning and cannot find an empty parking spot. I drive up and down the lanes and finally find a parking place. Ah, there's an empty spot. But wait, oh no, there's one of those rectangular signs with blue printing that says "15 MINUTE PARKING ONLY." Oh, sure I am going to get my shopping completed, stand in line for an open cashier, and load my own sacks in fifteen minutes. So that spot is no good.

I drive around some more and find another spot. Oops! Another sign reads, "EXPECTANT MOTHERS ONLY." I'm not expecting anything except to find a parking spot. That's the only thing I'm expecting at age eighty-seven. Been there and done that fifty years ago. And I don't remember seeing those signs when I was pregnant. And not this sign either, "MOTHERS WITH YOUNG CHILDREN." Where were all these signs when I needed them? The only sign was "DISABLED ONLY," which I wasn't in my child expecting/rearing/parking days. Now I could use a sign that reads "OLD BUT NOT DISABLED (yet)."

With all the signage, I wonder if the time will come when every parking spot will have its own sign. There would be one for "MALE DRIVER ONLY," which would lead to "FEMALE DRIVER ONLY." Why not differentiate by hair color: blondes, brunettes, bald, and so forth?

I accidentally found my solution. I wrenched my knee stepping in a hole in the pavement while walking a half mile to the front door of the grocery store after I found an empty spot in the parking lot of the pizza place next door.

Now I can truthfully use one of those designated disabled-only spots next to the front door. I reluctantly asked my doctor if she would sign my note that I am indeed disabled. I say reluctantly because I did feel guilty for asking, but she assured me that some of her patients in their fifties were asking for one. That assuaged my guilt a little.

As I limped into the lobby of the DMV with my doctor's note in hand, the young girl behind the desk said, "Here comes another one." I do wonder how many of those little blue disabled stickers she dispenses daily or weekly.

Anyway, to my credit, I try not to use or overuse my newfound parking privileges, if I can help it. I will look for a regular empty parking space unless it's raining, I'm in a hurry, or I'm feeling old.

Recommended reading: *Getting Older Better: The Best Advice Ever on Money, Health, Creativity, Sex, Work, Retirement and More* by Pamela D. Blair.

SPIT

Let's talk spit. I don't mean a sharp, pointed rod for roasting meat. I mean the stuff that is ejected from one's mouth, saliva or spittle, whatever you want to call it.

In the small town where I grew up, I would often notice the older men in overalls standing on the corners talking to one another. Between laughing about their week's projects and commenting on the weather, they would spit. It seemed the longer the projectile, the more in awe I was. How could they spit between their teeth and have it go so far? I never accomplished that feat. I could spit, but just a girl-spit, nothing spectacular. It was a little more than a dribble.

It seemed that spit was very much a part of our lives. We used spit on a lot of things. We'd spit on our hands and rub on the base of the bat when it was our turn to take a swing. Spit was used to find a leak in the inner rubber part of a bicycle tire. On boring, hot summer afternoons, spitting contests were held, usually on dry dirt just to make the spittle stand out, the idea being that the one who could spit the furthest was the winner. In my neighborhood, the champion spitter was not someone to be sneezed at.

Today we are still using spit but not realizing it. Ever try to open one of those plastic sacks in the grocery store without a little moisture on your hands? Several times I have given up and just dropped the bare-assed asparagus in the metal cart.

Trying to get cat hair off a pillow does require some moisture, or what we call spit on your hands.

The professional baseball commissioner recently declared spiting on a pitched ball as illegal. But it doesn't stop the players from spitting as they man their bases. And those pitchers can really put it out there. I mean, I don't know where they get all that spit. You'd think their mouths would be dry as toast by the end of the game.

Now it seems that the game of cricket has discovered spit. One cricketer has been quoted as saying, "As a practitioner, I just lick the inside of my forefinger, and it gives you a better grip on a cricket ball."

A committee of the International Cricket Council has recommended that the use of any moisture be banned. Apparently it is not cricket to slaver the ball with saliva. I am not a follower of professional cricket, but it may be worth watching just to catch the illegal activities of the cricketers. It just goes back to my original premise: spit is useful in many ways, legal or illegal.

To spit or not to spit, that is the question. As a female, I must say it just does not seem ladylike; however, if no one is looking, go ahead.

Believe it or not, there is a book about, yes, you guessed it, spit. See below.

Recommended reading: *Spit: What's Cool about Drool* by Mary Batten.

SAYING NO

As I write this, I am eighty-seven years old. I am not classified in the Greatest Generation, although I knew quite a few of the Greatest. Some were close relatives. They fought in World War II, and most came home safely. My part of the war effort was going door to door in my Girl Scout uniform asking the housewives for their discarded grease (from cooking) every Saturday morning. I was told that the grease would be used to make bombs. I also helped with paper drives.

While there aren't official generation definitions, I am classified as a member of the Silent Generation. It was impressed on us that we had to be generous and kind and never say no. That seems to have followed me all my life. I have a hard time passing up the poor homeless person sitting at the stoplight with her black-marker message scrolled across a torn piece of cardboard. I am especially kind to animals (note: four cats at this time).

But in this age of telemarketing, my aversion to saying no has reached a limit. If I get one more phone call trying to tell me I had won a cruise, credit card improvements, a new roof, and so forth, I will scream. I hate to say it, but I have become downright rude. Saying no is one thing but banging down the phone after running through the house to grab the phone and then hearing the lapse of time while they thumb through their written-out script before my newfound friend is going to give me a thrill of a lifetime. Silent no more! I may have lost my membership with the silent group.

And why do we have to be silent anyway? We have lived long lives, contributed to the goodness of humanity, paid our taxes, and voted in most political races, and we're still here. Apparently we have done something right.

Don't be afraid to say that two-letter word: No!

Recommended reading: *How to Say No Without Feeling Guilty: And Say Yes to More Time, More Joy and What Matters Most to You* by Patti Breitman and Connie Hatch.

ROBOTS ARE HERE TO STAY (MAYBE)

I don't usually fall for the new inventions, but those robotic sweepers seemed to have a lot of charm as well as being useful. After looking at several of those cute little sweepers, I found one at my price in a local big box store. I picked it up, lugged it home, and pulled all the pieces out of the box, and out fell a little yellow card. To my amazement, the little card was like a birth announcement. Apparently I was now the proud mother of a sweeper. The announcement read:

Date of birth: 8-29-16

Weight: 7 lbs.

Height: 32"

Plus, it/he came with a name. My new addition was named Bobi. I thought I was done giving birth to anything, never dreaming I would experience a late-in-life sweeper. I was beginning to have second thoughts about this unplanned addition to the family.

After recovering from my apparent birthing experience, I connected my sweeper to the electrical outlet and switched it on. This was going to be my answer to dragging out my heavy sweeper every day. (I have three cats.) Sweeping up the dust, cat hairs, and accumulated tinsel left over from some celebration was going to be a breeze. My little Bobi started whirling and twirling and sucking all the bad stuff out of the carpet.

According to all the convincing ads, this little jewel would sweep over the entire floor area and then all by itself return to its little garage. My robot didn't quite make it to its garage; in fact it didn't even make it to its driveway. It kind of stopped and groaned. Actually Bobi had missed half of the floor after bumping into every chair leg along the way. Like any good patient mother, I urged little Bobi into his garage. To be truthful, I actually shoved little Bobi into his resting position.

It turns out I am not such a good mother. "Failed at robotic motherhood" goes on my life's résumé. I felt terrible, but I decided to return Bobi to his original home, the box store. With a heavy heart, I boxed up the little guy, closed the lid, and drove off to the mall. I dragged the box to the return counter and explained to the girl that Bobi and I were apparently not meant for each other. I tried to avoid her disapproving eyes. I was strong to the end and walked away triumphant. Goodbye, Bobi. Maybe someday we will meet again. But I doubt it.

As for me, I have ridden my house of carpets, replacing them with tile floors. It's much easier to clean. I have reconnected with a nameless soft-bristled broom. Some days as I sit alone, I contemplate my life, both successes and failures, and wonder what became of Bobi. Hopefully he found a nice welcoming home who loved him and gave him lots of opportunity to roll around the house all day.

Some coupling was just not meant to be. Sorry, Bobi,

it was just one of those things. One of those crazy things. Thanks, Cole Porter.

Recommended reading: *Robotics: Everything You Need to Know about Robotics from Beginning to End* by Peter McKinnon.

TECH SPEAK

A new language has been created via emailing, smartphones, or chatting. Tech speak refers to abbreviations and acronyms used by computer techs, programmers, engineers, and just plain computer dummies. Tech speak is using acronyms instead of real words. Sometimes it is known as "disemboweling." Get it? No vowels. Acronyms such as LOL used to mean "lots of love." Now it means "laughing out loud." Usually these acronyms are written in capital letters. A whole paragraph can be written by using a lot of acronyms. Let's see if you could decipher this paragraph using most of the twenty common acronyms. There are some "real" words to help the story along. (The answers are at the end of the article.)

> FYI, IIRC you went FTW while debating your friend. SMH IMHO you could have been nicer. FWIW and TBH and TBF IRL you would not act like that. BTW ICYMI there is a new book relating to the situation. AFAIK this is not the only book on the subject. LMK if you agree. IDK we may LOL about it. NP we'll still be friends IKR? OMG, I hope I haven't hurt feelings. BFF?

Have we come to this? Communicating in acronyms? What happened to talking face-to-face, you know, the old-fashioned way when we looked each other in the eye and exchanged views out loud? Remember when we told our children to look at the person you are talking to, eye to eye. Now none of us practice it when we are texting, messaging, or leaving voice mail.

Let's talk about emoticons, also called emojis. When someone agrees with your point, you may get an owl emoji. If you are not familiar with the up-to-date emojis, there is a Semapedia website. You certainly would not want to send the wrong emotion like a real human.

GIFs are another way to avoid eye contact. GIFs are animated images that consist of cartoons or snippets of films. You can find a huge assortment of GIFs on sites such as Giphy, more emotionless pictures to be used as we become less human. Oh good, you can also make your own GIFs using online tools such as Giphy GIF Maker.

If you are completely confused, you can always pick up your phone and call someone. Remember how we dialed a phone and actually talked/spoke, you know, using real words and making an arrangement to meet a friend for lunch? Sit across from your friend, look each other in the eye, and exchange thoughts the old-fashioned way.

AN INTRODUCTION TO TECH SPEAK WORDS

- bot: A fake account run by a software application instead of a human.
- catfish: Someone who pretends to be someone they are not.
- fake news: Falsified news stories containing incorrect information.
- FOMO: Fear of missing out; anxiety when you see everyone having fun and you're not.
- humblebrag: A post of humility but a thin veneer of bragging.
- lurker: Someone who regularly reads messages but rarely contributes.
- thirst trap: A sexy photo posted on social media.

One word of caution: Never use an eggplant emoji. Don't ask me why. Look it up.

As senior citizens, we should try to keep up with the new jargon. Many books on the market will help you. As someone said, understanding tech speak doesn't need to be rocket science. We have conquered many obstacles in our lives; this too we will conquer.

- AFAIK: As far as I know.
- BFF: Best friend forever.
- BTW: By the way.

- FTW: For the win.
- FWIW: For what it's worth.
- ICYMI: In case you missed it.
- IDK: I don't know.
- IKR: I know, right?
- IMHO: In my humble opinion.
- IRL: In real life.
- ITRC: If I recall correctly.
- LMK: Let me know.
- LOL: Laugh out loud.
- NP: No problem.
- OMG: Oh my gosh.
- SMH: Shaking my head.
- TBF: To be fair.
- TBH: To be honest.

Book recommendations: *Kill Reply All: A Modern Guide to Online Etiquette from Social Media to Work to Love* by Victoria Turk and *Technology for Seniors* by David Peterka.

Q FOR QUARANTINE

Dear Grandchildren,

I know you are quizzical about what I did during the great quarantine of 2020 due to the COVID-19 pandemic. It was a unique time in the history of the country and my life's history. While pondering my pandemic productivity, I became interested in the word itself. Quarantine, it's an unusual word: *the isolation of persons, animals, ships, or goods infected by or exposed to an infectious disease.* Yes, that is us, stuck in the house, except for the cats who don't seem one bit affected by the isolation. As long as they get their two squares a day, they are happy cats.

Q is an unusual letter that is almost always followed by the letter U. How many words in our English language begin with a Q? There are only five pages of Q words in my favorite dictionary. But the poor letter X only has one page of useable words. But enough about Xs.

The Qs do offer some interesting words. Watch while I will attempt to use all. The ducks may quack, or are they emoting sounds of quackery? This may be a quagmire I've gotten myself into. I may not be qualified to explain qualitative analysis or even the quantum theory, but I have no qualms about identifying a quaint quail landing on some Queen Anne's lace in a quiet field.

I have visited Quito (capital of Ecuador) but never Quebec, Canada, or the country of Qatar in southwestern Asia but am in a quandary as to why I would even want to. However, I am interested in checking into Quincy, Massachusetts, in the future. I am not qualified to quarrel with a trip adviser who wanted to send me to Quezon City in the Philippines, but I find it questionable that she does not know that I get queasy about long flights. I may sound quarrelsome, but I quake with fear when I see the quantity of people boarding the plane ahead of me. It is quadruple the number I would desire.

When finally seated, I will quaff my fears and have no qualms of having another. While sitting in my first-class seat, I feel like a queen and enjoy my quietude. Luckily I don't have a seatmate the size of a quarterback. However, this has been quite exhausting, and I am feeling queasy but quiver at the thought of the queue of people deboarding the plane. And I am queerly puzzled at the number of bags they carry. Isn't there a quota?

So, dear grandchildren, don't ask me what I was doing during the quarantine of 2020. I was wasting time like everyone else. I was learning all the words that begin with Q and using them in a quasi-flight. I feel querulous about my questionable quirky behavior, but that is what happens when you are quarantined too long. With my quest to answer your query about my questionable sanity in my state of quiescence, I will quickly and quietly quantify my thoughts with two words: I quit!

Lovingly,
Your Quotable Grandmother

Recommended reading: Any dictionary. I know Siri is faster and so convenient, but a dictionary has so much more information.

PETS

I am a pet person and have been for as long as I can remember. We always had a cat and a dog in the household. Over the years, we have also had rabbits, a chicken, a snake, and a recalcitrant pony who became so obstreperous that we gave her back to the man who sold her to us. (I wonder how many times that man had "sold" that pony.)

My father also had hunting dogs. The hound dogs were kept outside but received excellent care and were fed regularly. They had doghouses that were comfortable in any weather. The female coon hounds were usually named Queenie, and the male dog was usually Duke. I learned from him that if you have an animal, you must take good care of it. This lesson must not have worn off because I have always thought of my pets as members of the family: they are well cared for, have food on demand, and have a safe and warm place to sleep.

Research says that pet owners are less likely to develop heart disease. And if one does have a heart attack, those who have a pet at home will live longer than those without. Some studies show that a pet's calming influence helps control blood pressure and stress.

At present, I have four cats. Don't ask why. The oldest cat must be thirteen years old by now. If cat years are the same as dog years compared to humans, he must be about my age. His name is Garfield and he is similar to the comic strip cat, as he has never relinquished his independence or insouciance.

He came out of the woods behind my house one day looking rather bedraggled, so I assumed he was feral. He has a tattoo in one ear, so I suppose he had been captured and spayed, but he never told me the details. I started leaving food on the patio for him. The more food he got, the friendlier he became.

I put a box on the front porch so he would have shelter and a warm place to sleep. I opened the front door one morning to see how he was liking his new accommodations. When he saw the open door, he ran into the house like a speeding bullet, made himself at home, and has been here ever since. Since he has become older, he no longer prowls the neighborhood but mostly stays in the yard when he ventures outside.

He is having a bit of trouble controlling his bladder. For some reason, he likes to pee on my shag throw rug in the bathroom. When I discover the wet rug, I hang it in front of him, and he admits his guilt by hanging his head and running for the door. Why he didn't run for the door before he peed on my rug, I will never know. I would like to stay mad at Garfield, but at my age, I am experiencing a little urine problem of my own. I haven't gone on the bathroom rug, but I came close a few times. Hey, at eighty years old, something has got to leak.

Enjoy your pets. They don't last forever, and yes, they do go to heaven.

Recommended reading: *Some Pets* by Angela DiTerlizzi.

CHOCOLATE CAKE

My grandson's birthday arrived. He had his heart set on a double chocolate cake that his cousin has every year on his birthday. The trouble is that that cake is only sold at a local box store, a box store for which one has to have a membership. Unfortunately, I don't have a membership, and I don't plan to purchase one just to buy one of their cakes.

Like a good grandmother, I called the big box store. After being transferred to five different departments (incidentally, the bakery didn't have an extension number), I talked to someone in the food court. The food court bigwig encouraged me to talk to someone in the administration office. I finally talked to someone with supposed authority. I asked if I could buy one of their famous chocolate cakes for my grandson.

The person on the phone gave me good news. "You don't have to have a membership to use our bakery." He advised that I tell the greeter at the front door that I was just there to use the bakery. That made sense to me, so off I went to the box store.

I was stopped at the door by a person whom I assumed was the greeter, who wanted to see my card. I assured him I was just there to buy a cake. He gave me directions to the bakery department, which turned out to be incorrect. However, I kept wandering around this huge store, dodging other purchasers with piled-high grocery carts. What did these people do with all that toilet paper?

I finally found the bakery department tucked in the back corner of the building. I saw no chocolate cakes, so I asked one of the clerks behind the bakery case. She assured me they had cakes, but they were still unfrosted. I said I would willingly wait for the twenty minutes, which turned out to be forty.

Finally, with cake in hand and no cart for me, I ventured toward the front of the store. I was still looking for the front when I stopped a man whom I thought was an employee of the store and asked where the checkout counter was. He was not too obliging and mumbled something about having a card. What is it with these people and their interest in my owning a card?

Without the help of that nonemployee, I found a checkout lane and put my cake on the counter, and a nice young employee asked if she could help.

I said, "Yes, I want to pay for this cake."

And she asked, "Where's your card?"

Geez, the card again. I said, "I do not have a card. I am just here to get a cake from your bakery."

And she politely replied, "No card, no cake."

Haven't I seen this episode on *Seinfeld*? I told the nice young woman that I had called the administration office and had been assured I did not need a membership to use the bakery.

She reiterated, "No card, no cake." She even offered to return the cake to the bakery.

That was nice of her, but I was not leaving the store without that damn cake. I told her I was eighty-seven years old, had driven a long distance, and was not interested in having a membership for sixty dollars just to purchase a cake. (And I already had enough toilet paper at home.)

She became so agitated that she called a manager who looked to be about twenty-one years old. I had to go through my sad story once again: eighty-seven years old, long drive, and no membership card.

He didn't know who had given me such bad advice about the no-membership departments and informed me the two departments I could use freely were the pharmacy and liquor, two departments that did not interest me a bit. He finally begrudgingly assented to let me purchase the cake. I paid, stuffed the receipt in my handbag, and walked toward the exit with cake in hand. Incidentally, there was no sack, just a cake encased in plastic.

I got in the long line at the exit door. An employee, I assume the exit-greeter, asked to see my receipt. So I had to get out of line, find a level area, set the cake down safely, and rummage through my handbag to find the receipt. So with receipt in hand, I was allowed to leave the store with my cake. Mission accomplished!

Recommended reading: *How to Say It to Seniors: Closing the Communication Gap with Elders* by David Solie.

WORKING LATE

I just saw on TV a blurb about a woman who was a hundred years old working at a McDonald's. Of course, all the announcers were oohing and aahing about this woman (who was actually ninety-nine years old by the way, not yet a hundred) who was still working. I didn't know if they were making fun of her or admiring her. Every time I see a blurb like this, "old person still working," it makes me a little irritated. In the near future, living to be a hundred will not be an anomaly. It will be the norm.

Wake up, people. You are going to be living longer than any preceding generation. I don't understand why everyone doesn't get it. There will be many people we now think of advanced age who will participating in life activities and, yes, working. Living to be a hundred years old will not be unusual.

You may retire at sixty-five, sixty-seven, or seventy, but there are many more working years ahead of you if you wish. My generation (the Silent Generation) grew up on work. We admired those around us who went out the door daily and put in eight hours of work. The thought then was to retire at age sixty-five and then die. But now, not so. Because of our newfound longevity, we could go on and create a whole new life after sixty-five—new ideas, new occupations, new adventures, and new worlds to conquer at any age.

Of course, the secret, or one of them, is good health.

That latest hundred-year-old heroine on TV that I saw did not look like a woman who had stacked up a hundred years. She moved and looked like she was in pretty good shape physically. Also she was mentally acute as she was manning the cash register and handing out change.

Practice good health. Practice moderation in everything you do, eat, and drink. Take part in physical activity of some kind at least thirty minutes a day or more. I know that is difficult to do especially if you haven't been physically active for a number of years. Start slowly, and if nothing else, walk every day. Striving for ten thousand steps a day may seem too much. Start with one step. You only have 9,999 to go. Start small but go for it.

As for me, I'm going out the door to look for a job. McDonald's, here I come.

Recommended book: *The Longevity Revolution: The Benefits and Challenges of Living a Long Life* by Robert N. Butler.

TREES

Take a walk. According to the Harvard Medical School, start the day by taking a stroll around your neighborhood. Being in nature can help lift your mood. Whether it is spending ten minutes on your porch or actually striding the sidewalks, you can be inspired by nature if you take the time to really look around. To make it more enjoyable, look for an area with trees. Trees are magnificent creatures. Tall, short, and fat, they are wonderful to just admire.

Get up close and personal with a tree. They are like humans, living creatures just like us. They have branches;

we have limbs. Like human families, tree parents live with or near their children, communicate with them, and share nutrients. They grow, produce, age, and die.

Trees provide cooling shade, attract birds, purify our air, and prevent soil erosion. Trees also add grace and beauty to our homes and communities. And they never tell their ages. Or do they? To determine the age of a tree:

1. Measure the circumference of a tree at a point four and a half feet above the ground.
2. Divide this measurement by 3.14 (pi). This is the diameter at breast height.
3. Research the estimated yearly growth of your tree (oak, elm, elder, etc.).

The growth number times the diameter is the age of the tree.

Just a little tree trivia from the Arbor Day Foundation:

- Fifty million people rely on forests for clean drinking water in the United States.
- Baseball bats are made of wood from an ash tree.
- Most tree seedlings grow at a rate of six inches a year.
- There are 850 species of trees in the United States.
- An average American will use seven trees each year in paper, wood, and other tree products.
- The oldest tree in the United States is 4,800 years old.

Stop and inspect a tree branch closely, and you will be surprised to see how many Ys are on a branch. Every branch is filled with our English letter Y. That bit of trivia of Americans using seven trees per year makes me wonder if the tree is asking "Why?" in the form of a Y. *Why* are you chopping down so many of my wonderful relatives? *Why* do you need so many of my tree cousins? *Why* don't you give us trees more respect?

You may find yourself looking at a tree differently. If the neighbors find you talking to a tree and they give you a quizzical look, just say, "Yes, I am communicating with a tree, and you should try it too."

If there is a nature center in your area, make a point to visit. Get acquainted with the people in charge. Ask questions about the fauna in your neighborhood. In any case, get outside, explore nature, and introduce yourself to the beauty of the trees. Make friends with a tree.

Recommended reading: *Hidden Life of Trees, What They Feel, How They Communicate* by Peter Wohllenben.

CORONAVIRUS

———— ◦ ————

Aren't you glad you're old? We of a certain age have lived through five wars (one cold), three revolutions, numerous movements, several cycles of crisis, and a couple of solar eclipses. A virus blackout is a new challenge. Nor have we ever been quarantined, at least not since the scarlet fever days with red signs on the doors.

Just when we thought we had seen everything, along comes the coronavirus. And to add insult to injury, this virus seems to be attracted to our age group (old). We had been defined as the Silent Generation. But apparently we weren't silent enough to escape this strange little virus.

We were warned to stay in the house, wash our hands every five minutes with special soap, and drink lots of water. Wear a mask when you have to leave the house. Gloves are recommended, and bacterial wipes should be used to wipe down anything within arm's length. Toilet paper suddenly disappeared off all grocery shelves almost overnight. Someday that will be explained. But for now, it remains an enigma. That may be mentioned in wills: *I bequeath my closet full of toilet paper to my children to be distributed evenly among my living heirs.*

We have been inundated with new phrases that deal with this virus and how we were supposed to live with it or at least escape its venom, such as:

- Stop the spread: This does not refer to hip size.
- Shelter-in-place: Why does this remind me of something a veterinarian would say?
- Social distancing: Don't talk, sit close, or hug anyone except your cat, another vet intervention.
- New normal: What's normal? Let's hope the new normal is more exciting.
- Don't touch your face: I avoid mirrors, so why would I want to acknowledge more of those facial wrinkles?
- Stay home: And do what? Exercise?
- Isolation encouraged: No problem there. I'll exercise alone. Not!
- Flatten the curve: Now this one really befuddles me. What, where, and whose curve?

And frankly, if I hear "We're in this together," I am going to throw up.

Anyway, folks, we will get through this. I would encourage you to write down your thoughts in these trying times. If you haven't journaled before, now is the time to start. It will be an interesting historic note in your family tree. Your ancestors will be curious about your feelings during the coronavirus of the year 2020. The virus probably will be a once-in-a-lifetime occurrence, possibly a once-in-a century occurrence. The good news is that you have lived through it.

Recommended reading: *5-Minute Happiness Journal* by Leslie Marchand.

HALF-PRICED MAN

⸺⸺⸺⸺⸺ ✒ ⸺⸺⸺⸺⸺

I had a friend whom I called the Half-Priced Man. He was married and had a job, house, and family. He was not a teenager living at home in his father's basement. However, he did have an unusual connection to his father. At least I had never heard of this father/son connection before. My friend went through life paying half price for everything. His father paid for half of everything he purchased.

Apparently they had made some kind of arrangement that whatever he bought, his father would pay half. Obviously he and his father were very close, compatriots, companions, or whatever you want to call it. So when my friend bought a house, his father paid for half. When he bought a truck, his father paid for half. When he bought some acreage in the country, his father paid half. I always wanted to ask my friend how he had made this arrangement with his father. I wondered if I could make the same deal with my father. In fact, I tried.

He replied, "Are you nuts? You want it; you pay for it."

I was still intrigued with this half-price way of living. I thought, *How wonderful.* I myself love a good sale. I once heard a woman say she never bought anything on sale. I, on the other hand, purchase most items on sale.

So I wanted to turn to her and say, "You have found your other half, so to speak. You pay full; I pay half, if possible."

But she didn't look as if she would appreciate my sense of humor.

To go through life at half-price is not to be sneered at. I actually envied my half-priced friend. I have read articles that encourage bargaining. Ask the clerk if she could knock off a few bucks. I tried it, but it just didn't work for me. I'm not too persuasive. It kind of goes along with my salesmanship ability. "You don't really want this, do you?" Obviously I wasn't a successful salesperson, probably one of the many reasons I became a librarian. My library books are free. I don't need any salesmanship there. You either want the book or you don't. The best part is there's no charge.

Anyway, if you want to live a half-priced life, you may try it. It might work for you. You'd better have a father who goes along with it. As for me, I will wait for a good sale.

Recommended book: *Live Life for Half Price* by Mary Hunt.

REAL ESTATE

I have a subscription to a national newspaper at this time. I don't know how long I will continue, but for now I appreciate the content. This newspaper covers business and world news, technology, sports, arts, and much more. On some weekend editions, it also lists real estate for sale, valuable real estate, that is. Prices vary from $730,000 to $3,495,000.

The least expensive (and I hate to use the word "cheapest" because it sounds so maudlin) real estate listed was a mere $500,000. This pittance would cover the price of a lake in the middle of Minnesota with a small cabin included. It was probably a cabin used by some old ice fishermen who used it for a "fun, rollicking" weekend in the middle of winter, freezing cold. I am assuming there is a potbelly stove in the middle of the cabin providing the heat and the required hole in the floor for dropping a fishing line in the lake while the lucky owner of this paradise is hugging the potbelly stove to keep from being frozen to death in the middle of Minnesota.

These real estate ads are the most interesting layouts in the paper. The wording used to describe the real estate is spectacular. If there is an award for the most alluring sales pitches, these writers would take top prizes. Here is some of the wonderful prose describing my "cheap" lake property:

> This property provides gentle rolling topography
> and lovely sunrises and sunsets. Excellent hunting

retreat. Many trails for hiking, horseback riding, or four-wheeling. Ten minutes from world-class golf, dining, and resort accommodations.

In the first place, if it is just minutes from world-class golf and resort accommodations, why don't I just go there instead of some dirty, drafty cabin used on weekends by some equally dirty, drafty old fisherman?

Here is an ad for a home in southern California that is so expensive that the price isn't even listed. Apparently if you want to make a bid, there is a phone number and an email address to submit your bid. There is a due date, so if you are interested, get on it! This ad has a photo of the home, and the home and all the outbuildings cover half a hillside. This ad reads:

> Spectacular 360-degree view, superb amenities, secluded location, custom designed/new construction, 4 bed, 4.5 bath, 5,500-square-feet home. Also features an infinity lap pool, built-in jacuzzi, underground wine cave, outdoor shower, attached and detached garages.

It sounds tempting, but I don't know about that *infinity lap pool*. How much infinity is involved in a lap pool? And about that *outdoor shower*, if I have to go outside to take a shower, I'm really not interested.

I guess I will stay in my little house, 1,200 square feet, three bedrooms, and spectacular view of backyard woods. It's small but adequate; however, I do have an indoor shower.

In fact, I have two indoor showers. So good luck selling your grand home in southern California. I'm sure you will find a buyer who will purchase it, love it, and enjoy the house into infinity and beyond.

Recommended reading: *The Perfect Home* by Mary Gilliatt.

LIAR

Liar, liar, pants on fire. Remember when "liar" was not a name you wanted to be called. There was a time when being called a liar was as bad as that A on Prim's chest. But now it seems everyone, and I mean politicians, want-to-be politicians, and hangers-on seem to enjoy lying. And why not? There seem to be no consequences if you are caught telling an untruth. A falsehood is seemingly not the sin it once was.

Mirrors don't lie, but politicians do. Our first president, George Washington, admitted his lie when he 'fessed up to chopping down that cherry tree. I don't know what his consequences were at the time but hopefully enough of a punishment to leave the rest of the trees alone. But just think how that story about George has survived over two hundred years. It made such a mark on history that it is still told. Just because he told a lie.

Politicians, take note. Our first president told a lie, got caught, and took his punishment. In today's world of politicians, they tell enough falsehoods to have whole books written about them. Unfortunately, today even if they get caught, which is rare, there is no pointing a finger and labeling them "Liar!" or better yet, "Liar, liar pants on fire."

Unfortunately we constituents have short memories. One of the greatest assets of a politician is our short memories or our lack of not following up and checking the facts, true facts. But what are we going to do about it if we do hear a politician telling a lie on TV? Yell at the TV? That falls on deaf ears. I can write to my congressmen and explain that maybe he should check the record on that story. By the time my missile reaches his hand, if it ever does, he has moved on to another story filled with made-up facts.

It seems lying is not in anyone's vernacular anymore. Lying is now called untruths or post-truths. It has been noted that politicians are professional liars or, as the writer George Orwell put it, "Political language ... is designed to make lies sound truthful."

And that's no lie.

ROBOCALLS

How are you fixed for robocalls? If you are like me, you have had enough. Enough already!

I have just had a call from Sally. I immediately hung up when I realized it was just another one of those calls. But Sally is persistent and calls again. No, I don't know Sally, but she was very friendly and helpful but apparently has not kept up with my life. Sally wanted to help me reduce my student loans. I guess Sally has forgotten that I am eighty-seven years old. Time flies between friends.

As a matter of fact, I never had any student loans. My college career began at age forty-seven years old. Obviously I am a late bloomer. I signed up for one class at a junior college close to my home in northern Indiana. I was lucky enough to have a nun for my first college class. Sister Mary Delores convinced me that I should continue taking classes with the idea of becoming a college graduate. That was something I had never thought of, but one does what the Sister says, no matter what age, yours or hers. So I took one class at a time, one foot in front of the other, and lo and behold, thirteen years later while working full-time and tending a sick husband, I had a master's degree in library science from Indiana University. Thanks to Sister Mary Delores encouraging me along the way.

Back to Sally and all the faceless people who call me with the good news that I have won a free cruise, please stop. I have my number on a no-call list, but apparently the telemarketers have found holes in the list.

One of the most troubling and dangerous calls I have received is the one about my granddaughter. After my initial hello, the caller says, "Grandma, it's me." And I immediately fall into the trap and say, "Hi, Susie. (This caller does sound like my granddaughter.) What's the matter?"

She proceeds to tell me that because of some bad choices, she is in jail in Florida and desperately needs over a thousand dollars right away so she can be released. (And by the way, don't tell anyone else in the family.) After a few more platitudes, it dawned on me that the whole family, including Susie, had been in Florida a week ago, so why would she be there again? Lights go off, and bells ring. I realize I was almost duped into sending money to a total stranger posing as my granddaughter.

If you get such a call, do not send money until you get off the phone, make some calls to relatives, and ensure this is a real problem. Or you can do what I did when I got a similar desperate call about my grandson from a supposed jailer in Ohio.

"Oh no, my grandson is in jail? You can keep him. He's yours." Click! A fast hang-up. (Sorry, Jim.)

Recommended reading: *Don't Get Mad at Telemarketers, Get Even: How to Stop Those Annoying Calls* by Denny Chu.

MEMORIZE

To keep your brain sharp, you should memorize something every day. This is one of the secrets of keeping your brain awake and your memory functioning, according to *Almanac of Life Secrets and Tips*. To our credit, those of us living in the twenty-first century already memorize a lot of numbers. Think of just some of the numbers you know by heart: your Social Security number, addresses, phone numbers, PINs, and so forth. Our generation has probably committed more numbers to our daily lives than any previous generation.

If you want to add to your memory skills and impress a friend, find a poem and memorize it. Keep track of how long it takes you to be able to recite the first stanza. A good (easy) poet to start would be Henry Wadsworth Longfellow. Longfellow was called the children's poet for a good reason because most of his poems rhyme. An interesting poem to start with is "Paul Revere's Ride."

> Listen, my children and you shall hear
> of the midnight ride of Paul Revere.

I am sure you have heard of this poem. Everyone knows the immortal lines,

> One, if by land, and two, if by sea;
> And I on the opposite shore will be.

It is a rather long poem, fifteen stanzas in all, but learning the first two stanzas would be impressive.

Speaking of poems and memorization, over the years I have had this somewhat disturbing recurring recollection of being in the third grade taught by Miss Kelley. She assigned her third-grade class to memorize a poem, "Abdou Ben Ahom" by Leigh Hunt. Her instructions were to memorize this poem and later recite it before the whole room of non-poetic classmates. I worked on that poem for weeks, reading and reciting until I drove my mother, father, and brother nuts walking around the house talking about old Abou. Even the dog left the room.

I was finally ready to give my recitation. The next day when Miss Kelley asked the class who was ready to get up and give it a try, my hand shot up. I was going to be the first third grader to break through the memorization wall. I walked to the front of the room and stood proudly beside Miss Kelley's desk. She turned to me and said those immortal words, "OK, Marie, let's hear it."

I thought I had that poem permanently etched in my brain. I had practiced all that time. But suddenly with all my classmates staring at me, I went blank … totally blank. I couldn't remember the first line, to say nothing of the other eighteen lines. To say nothing is what I did.

The embarrassing silence must have transfixed Miss Kelley. We just stared at each other. It seemed like an eternity but probably only minutes. Those were some of the longest minutes in my short life.

Miss Kelley finally said more immortal words, "Marie, take a seat."

I slouched back to my middle-row desk. A front-row desk would have been easier and fewer steps to cover my embarrassment.

Funny thing, I ran across that poem in my later years (seventies). I added memorization of "Abou Ben Ahem" as one of my goals. I say with conviction, I can now recite the whole eighteen lines. Miss Kelley would be so proud.

Actually it is an interesting poem. I realize now it is a religious poem. In third grade, I had no idea what it was about. I learned it phonetically. I do think it was a bit much for a third-grader. Do teachers even assign poetry recitation these days? I doubt it.

Boy, my third grade was not a good year. I must have been happy to move on to fourth grade. I'm sure Miss Kelley was glad to see me go.

Recommended reading: "The Love Song of J. Alfred Prufrock" (a poem) by T. S. Eliot.

BALANCE

———————— ⟨≋⟩ ————————

I was reading an article about a middle-aged woman taking up rollerblading. Apparently the resurgence of rollerblading is happening. In another decade (sixties), I took up rollerblading. My husband gave me my first (and last) pair of Rollerblades as a birthday gift at age sixty-five. He had given up with the question of, "What next?"

I confess that I had a few short years of fulfilling my dreams as a roller derby queen. However, after an out-of-control downhill roll from which I had no other way of stopping except falling over, I had second thoughts of Rollerblade queenhood. Luckily it was a grassy area, so there were no broken bones, just loss of some dignity. Hurtling down an unexpected incline brought me to my senses. Being on eight wheels without any kind of braking power awakens one to one's immortality. So after getting back on my feet, or rollers, which incidentally is about as easy as getting upright on skis, I reluctantly but happily tucked my Rollerblades into a cabinet in the garage and closed the door on my in-line skating adventure.

What caught my eye was the quote the new roller blader said about her experience of rollerblading after landing flat on her back, "After having three kids, my balance is not what it used to be."

Whoa! In the first place, I didn't know I could blame my kids (four) for falling over on my Rollerblades. Plus, this opens the door for any other athletic deficiencies I admit to in my life, of which I have plenty. I can't swim well, my skiing sucks, and my golfing is too far over par to mention. My complete exercise program is suspect and leaves a lot to be desired. But I can always blame that fourth kid.

According to the newspaper article, people are so bored that they may think they can outroll over their boredom on wheels. But take it from me: it's not as easy as it looks. Once you are on those eight wheels, you are on your own. You may impress the neighbors on a smooth surface, but watch out for the inclines, big or small.

Incidentally, if you are looking for a pair of Rollerblades to try, I have a pair in my garage that you can use, practically new with low miles.

I too have noticed that my balance is not what it used to be. There are some exercises we elders can use to improve our balance. The recommending reading may be helpful.

Recommended reading: *Exercises for Better Balance: The Stand Strong Workout for Fall Prevention and Longevity by* William Smith.

TRYING TO BECOME A VIKING

MONUMENT

The year 2020 will surely be remembered as a monumental year. The history books may register 2020 as a year of many things, such as a vicious coronavirus, quarantines, shelter-in-place, disrupted lives, and also a hard year on monuments. This is the year of transfer of, removal of, or just plain destruction of many of our country's national monuments, also known as statues. It would seem to me that it takes a lot of strength to knock down a large piece of iron that has been attached to another large piece of an iron base for a hundred years. I may walk with the protesters, but don't ask me to knock down a statue that has been standing there eons before my birth, which, by the way, makes those statues pretty old.

The living things that have enjoyed those many statues the most are the birds, especially the pigeons. If anyone has a gripe, it seems to me it must be the birds. Did anyone stop and ask our feathered friends if it is OK to remove some of their resting/pooping areas? I bet not.

Mr. Sparrow says to Mrs. Sparrow, "I'm going down to Robert E. Lee's and relieve myself and talk to old man woodpecker for a while."

And Mrs. S. thinks, *Good riddance. He's driving me nuts since he retired.*

Unlike the birds, I hardly looked at the statues, huge objects I would walk by and not even notice. Does anyone really look at those old statues? Come on. Be truthful. I'll bet the monument destroyers never even noticed those statues of historic note before they started to yank on the rope to behead the horse and dethrone the general of some forgotten battle of some forgotten war. Those statue-destroyers probably slept through that history lesson, if they attended class at all.

I loved history class (minority of one); however, even I am not a big gawker or appreciator of old statues. It is just something that has always been on the corner, kind of like a water hydrant, but less useful and not painted yellow.

Washington, D.C. Is loaded with statues and monuments of all kinds. I had the opportunity to visit our capital city with a group of high school kids. With kids, it was a rule to visit all the historic sights whether they wanted to or not. It was my chance to see up close and personal the historic figures of our country's past. Of course, that included the impressive Washington Monument, the Lincoln Memorial, Tomb of the Unknown Soldier, and more.

The one statue, or group of statues, that was the most moving to me was the group of nineteen large iron soldiers representing the Korean War. The designers were Frank Gaylord and Louis Nelson, and it was established in 1995.

The Vietnam Veterans Memorial, designed by Maya Lin and opened in 1982, is truly an architectural achievement. And try knocking that one over. It has turned out to be a place for sad remembrances and grieving hearts as well as a place to talk to your lost sons, brothers, and unknown grandfathers and leave personal mementos. Maybe we should have erected walls all along, walls to represent our history and all the fallen servicepeople who gave their lives for our country.

Incidentally, when the memorial was first opened, it

was not received well. There was a lot of consternation and grumbling about that. "A wall? Where's the horse and rider?" As it turned out, the Vietnam Veterans Memorial is the most visited statue in Washington, D.C. with six million visitors a year. And for some visitors, it is the most meaningful.

If you have a chance to visit our nation's capital, be sure to visit and enjoy our historic landmarks and appreciate the people who designed, executed, and erected the statues. Also take time to visit the statues in your own town. It may be the first time you have really looked at and appreciated their monumental beauty. They may be gone tomorrow.

Recommended reading: *Museums, Monuments, and National Parks: Towards a New Genealogy of Public History* by Denise D. Meringolo.

POLITICIANS

I have finally figured out the political scene. It didn't take long, just eighty-plus years. It is all a game. Why didn't I see this before? The game of chess comes into mind, but the present politicians are not that intelligent. Maybe Monopoly since money flows freely. Lobbyists are throwing money around like crazy. Or the game of Clue? I don't believe that most of the present politicians even have a clue, certainly not a hint of what their constituents really want.

Politicians are thinking, *What is the next move? Should I run locally or regionally? Run now or wait until 2024, 2028, and so on? If the current president fails—and he is most likely and I have railed against him—I'll be in a good position to win votes for being so farsighted. I didn't ever like or approve of him. Chess moves extraordinaire. Game point won.*

The winner gets their name in the history books if they are lucky enough to win many terms for future generations to read about, and historians who are really interested in the so-called winners will write books about, discuss widely, and pretend to understand their beings.

The state of today's national politicians has no interest in their bosses, otherwise known as constituents (that is, us folks). Once they get in office, they can do almost anything they desire. Who cares? No one is looking. Actually it's not a bad gig. They surround themselves with aides that probably know more about the issues than they do. Or else the aides wouldn't be put on the payroll. They would not even be considered.

The vacation days almost outnumber their working days, and then after flimflamming their constituents, those addled brained folks at home, they can retire with all the benefits they have enjoyed during all those glorious days in the Senate or House of Representatives. I don't think our Founding Fathers, the ones that our politicians like to compare themselves to during election time, did not consider the political offices as lifetime jobs.

But not so in today's world. Look at the ages of some of our politicians, the ones who get on TV and then cannot read the prescribed script one of the above-mentioned brainy aides had carefully typed out in enlarged bold letters for his boss to read. And even then, the aged politician still stumbles and guffaws their way through the text.

Let's not even mention all the vacations the politicians take. But I would like to mention term limits. If the president is limited to two terms, why not the representatives?

So what can we the voters do about our present predicament of the profundity of poor politicians? Never skip an election. It is your duty to cast your vote. Wars are fought to protect our right to vote. Remember those who have come before you who have fought in those wars. Vote!

Recommended reading: *What You Need to Know About Voting and Why* by Kim Wehle.

NOT MUSICAL

I must be the most non-musical person in the world. In my next life, I am demanding that I can appreciate music. Please give me an ear to appreciate all the notes on the scale. I always wanted to be a band singer. To look like Doris Day and sing like Anita O'Day would be my ideal. Yes, I did like and enjoy Stan Kenton at one time. But when he died, not Buddy Holly, is when the music died for me. Sorry, "American Pie," but this works for me.

I was never a good singer. I was the only girl in eighth grade who was not asked to try out for the spring musical. I would like to blame my dropping out of the music world when I could no longer understand rap lyrics. Or worse, when I finally did decipher them, I was not a fan of what I was hearing. What happened to censorship or at least decency? Those lyrics are embarrassing, or am I just showing my eighty-seven years of puritanism? Frank Sinatra, Mel Torme, or Nat King Cole gave us lyrics that one could listen to and enjoy without getting red in the face.

I saw the musical group Earth, Wind, and Fire on TV the other day. They were being presented with an award for their contributions to the music world. I decided I would go to the library and pick up a record (oops, now called a CD) and reawaken or at least unblock my non-musical ear. I spend a lot of time in the local library since I am a retired librarian but have never checked out a musical CD. I had to ask the librarian how to find my desired CD. She was most helpful, as most librarians are. She picked out a CD that contained all of Earth, Wind, and Fire hits. She then assured me after listening to the greatest hits that I "would be groovin' all day."

After playing the CD in my car, I realized I was doing a lot of body motions that I hadn't done in a while. My movements may not be described as grooving, but I was sure feeling the beat of the music. Don't know if you call it groovin', but I appreciate the music of Earth, Wind, and Fire. And whatever award they are given is one for which they deserve. And that is coming from someone who certainly knows her music. Not!

But I am working on it. Next time I will be more dangerous and get the latest hits of the Beatles.

Recommended reading: *The Story of Music: How Music Has Shaped Civilization* by Howard Goodall.

DISCONNECTEDNESS

I am so tired of going somewhere, anywhere, and the people around me are looking at their palms (smartphones). We are being described as Palm People no matter the age, young, middle-aged, or old. While waiting for friends in a lobby of a restaurant, I noticed everyone, including the older patrons, were looking at their laps. Why are we so desperately locked into instant communication?

Comical happenings are being reported of people looking at their phones as they walked down a busy street. Some have walked into glass partitions. Serious accidents are occurring and causing bodily harm, all because people are not watching where they are going. They are too busy checking their emails.

I thought I was the only old person who was worried about this dangerous happening when I voiced my displeasure to a young girl. She too agreed that there is too much of turning off to our surroundings. She made a remarkable statement, "I want to be where my feet are."

Bingo! She summed it up prophetically. Be aware of where you are, where your feet are planted. Enjoy the world around you. Look at the other human beings in your vicinity. Mother Nature offers many lovely sights—lovely blue sky, green grass, and trees in blossom. Or communicate in the old-fashioned way, talking to one another.

There are studies being conducted by experts in the field

about disconnectedness, but let's not get scientific. Just enjoy where you are.

Recommended reading: *Enjoying Life: Making a Difference* by Elspeth Jackman.

TRAVEL, TRAVEL, TRAVEL

I started traveling in my seventies and made and met a goal of visiting all of the continents, which I have done now, except Antarctica, which is out of my budget. I realized I had missed some of the countries I had intended to visit. Within the last five years (before the pandemic and restrictions on travel), I had the opportunity to visit England and Scotland, Italy, Iceland, and the Scandinavian countries of Denmark, Norway, and Sweden.

The following articles describe in small details my experiences in all of these countries. All countries are different and alike in many ways. As a traveler, you will discover this contradiction for yourselves.

Do not let the price of traveling deter you. You can always find a travel tour with your price and your time limit, especially now when there are so many different tour groups. I have met many solo travelers in the last few years, so don't be fearful of traveling alone. You will meet new friends that will become lifelong friends.

ENGLAND

ENGLAND

STONEHENGE ENGLAND

England, Scotland, and Wales sounded like an interesting trip. I have been lost in most cities I have visited, and so why not get lost in London? And that is what I did. But before I got lost in London, I got left, left behind, that is. Our group was large with a well-informed guide. However, in London we were given to a local guide, as so often happens on these tours. The local guides are well-versed in local affairs. Our London guide took all us to Buckingham Palace along with hundreds of other tour groups. The palace grounds were packed with tourists. Did I mention that our London guide was short and carrying an umbrella, an umbrella that was not open? So all that was sticking up with this huge crowd was an unopened umbrella. It was really not much to follow.

When the festivities of the changing of the guard was over, crown dispersing, I could not find my group and had lost sight of the short guide. I did bump into another lady I recognized from our group, who also had a frantic look on her face. I convinced her I was one of the same tour group. She luckily had her cell phone with her, so when she got disconnected from her husband, she could call him and ask for help. He soon located us. I was as glad to see him as she was.

No one even looked for us. Did anyone know we were lost? Not so. It's another reason to carry a card from your hotel when you are out. Even with your group, it is easy to get lost in a strange city.

It did happen that my newfound friends were going to Churchill War Rooms, which had been recommended to visit. We had an interesting tour of the war rooms, and I too would recommend for everyone visiting London to make it one of your stops, to see and walk through the small rooms where Churchill stayed during a good part of World War II, especially to see the actual code breaker that helped the Allies bring the war to an end.

There is so much to see in London that it is difficult to mention all the sights. However, beware of the traffic. They not only drive on the "wrong" side of the road, but in London, the drivers drive very fast. You can imagine the amount of traffic.

As I parted from the couple, I thought I would walk back to the hotel. Dusk was setting in, so I did have to move along. Instead of taking a taxi, I thought I would walk back, not realizing how far our hotel was from the palace area. I set off but was confused about the direction. I stopped many Londoners along the way and asked if they could point me in the right direction. The longer I walked, getting darker every minute, the more I realized I was indeed lost. I finally got my bearings and finally found my hotel in the dark.

While traveling north in England, we visited Shakespeare's birthplace, Anne Hathaway's thatched cottage, and impressive Stonehenge. We saw hikers making their way on what Castle in Edinburgh. Driving back to London on the western edge of England, we passed through the lovely countryside. London was fast, but driving through the Lake District, I found was much more to my liking. And I discovered that England does have mountains.

I was not a Beatles fan, but it was interesting to visit the Cavern where the Beatles got their start. It was three flights down to the cave with lots of memorabilia on the walls.

Marie Albertson

The other women traveling alone made great companions, one of the friendliest group I had the pleasure of meeting. I still hear from some of them. And that is what happens when you travel alone. You make worldwide friends.

ITALY

———————————— ⌁ ————————————

I had traveled to many places since I had set the goal to visit every continent. I had visited Egypt, China, Australia, and so forth, but Italy was not on my list. I don't have anything against pizza and spaghetti, but Italy did not hold a fascination for me as much as other countries. So to round out my European tours, I booked a trip to Italy in the middle of November. As it turned out, November was a good time to miss some of the crowded tourist areas.

We landed in Rome. Once I met the other members of the tour in the hotel lobby, a new friend from Phoenix and I jumped on a local tour bus and took a quick trip around Rome. I knew we would be on the move most of the trip, so this would give me an opportunity to see Rome and view what most tourists go to see. We zipped past St. Peter's, the Vatican, Colosseum, and many more museums.

The next morning, we got on our touring bus. We passed through small villages and green farmlands. The rolling hills looked so peaceful. We arrived in Florence, which offers many attractions, the first being Michelangelo's marble statue of David. We had our own guide in the museum, who gave us a glowing history of the statue.

That evening we had a hosted meal. Most of the tours offer a hosted meal one time during your trip. In Italy, we were driven to an old house three hundred years old and visited with an Italian family. The hostess was a chef, so the food was exceptionally delicious. It is always nice to meet a local family. It gives us tourists an opportunity to ask questions and really get to know a local family.

The next morning, we were back on our bus, this time driving through San Gemignani. We stopped briefly to snap a photo of the Leaning Tower of Pisa, still standing and still leaning.

We spent another night in Florence. I would like to say I never got lost in Italy (as I have in other cities), but alas one night I was walking through the business area after leaving our hotel and then found myself a little lost. The area was having a small open-air shopping area, so people filled the streets. I asked a lot of people for directions to my hotel and finally found my way to the hotel.

It's a good time to remind you. If you are in a city in which you are not familiar, always take a card from your hotel if you go for a walk. It is very easy to become confused on streets in which you are not familiar. Even an envelope with a motel's return address is helpful.

On the way to Sienna, one late evening we stopped at the American Cemetery and Memorial. Four thousand white crosses stand at attention in the early evening mist, a most impressive sight. We were the only tourist group visiting at the time. The quietness and reverence were something special to remember about Italy.

Sienna puts on a horse race once a year that is quite spectacular. The horses are covered in robes denoting their tribes or groups. There are no rules, just an all-out horse race. The whole town gets involved in the race.

We stopped in Verona, the city in which Shakespeare's play

Romeo and Juliet took place. We viewed the famed balcony from which a fictional Juliet once called to her Romeo.

While driving north toward the Alps, the landscape changes dramatically—no more rolling hills and no more flat landscape. In the city of Bolzano, we visited the museum that houses Otzi, a frozen man that was found in 1991 in the Alps. He is a relic of the Stone Age, deemed to be five thousand years old. The skeleton of the man has been restored and kept in an air-conditioned room for all to view through a small window. His fingers are intact considering his age. It's very interesting. He was named Fritz because he was found in the Austrian Alps. The Italians with their unique sense of humor have renamed him Frozen Fritz.

The weather turned cold the closer we got to the Dolomites and the Alps. We drove on to Innsbruck, Austria, a beautiful city surrounded by the Alps.

Our last stop was in Venice, the city of canals, a city with four hundred bridges but no streets. The well-dressed gondoliers were in full regalia, but the weather had turned too cool for a boat ride. From there, we were taken by boat to the nearest airport. We then boarded a plane and started home.

Italy was a surprise to me, a pleasant surprise. The country offers many contrasts, which makes it a most interesting trip. I don't usually l say I would return to a country I had already visited, but Italy may be a country I would like to revisit.

ICELAND

ICELAND WATERFALL

RIDING SMALL HORSES IN ICELAND

Iceland is a land of ice, but not so. Icelanders started that rumor to keep non-Icelanders out. Apparently it is not working. Next year, two million visitors will invade Iceland, the size of Kentucky. Keep in mind that the native population is less than 400,000. So how these visitors will be taken care of may be a problem. Standing room only may be the key.

All of a sudden, Iceland seemed a desired destination on a lot of travelers' list of "Must Visit Before I Die." I was one of them. After a delayed flight from Chicago, we arrived in Iceland late of course, so our appointed tour guide had left the airport and driven back to Reykjavik. The airport in Iceland is about forty-five minutes from the capital. Luckily two other late arrivals from my tour also happened to be stranded at the airport. They were smart enough to keep all the tour information on their person and not in a suitcase stored somewhere not known to man or woman, like I did. Another good tip while traveling, keep important phone numbers and other travel information readily available.

They whipped out the telephone numbers of someone at the tour office back in America. Voilà! We were going to be picked up by an employee of the tour in a short time and delivered to our hotel. Hotel Husafell, here we come!

It turned out we would be eating our meals at the hotel when we were not out in the hinterlands. And that brings up the cost of food in Iceland. There are a few times when you are on your own for meals. Food is very expensive, so if you plan to visit Iceland, bring plenty of snacks or a jar of peanut butter. The two meals we ate in the hotel were $50 apiece. The buffet was good, but a peanut butter sandwich would have much less expensive.

The drive from the airport into town was interesting. The terrain made up of black lava rock was otherworldly. It was almost a moonscape feeling and totally desolate, still vestiges of the 2010 eruption of Eyjafjallajokull, which canceled two-thirds of European air travel for six days.

There are over a hundred waterfalls in Iceland, and the few I saw were breathtakingly spectacular. Godafoss, called the Waterfall of the Gods, is not the tallest waterfall, but it is the one pictures in all the Iceland brochures and lives up to its name.

I have visited many countries, but Iceland was the most unique. If you wanted to take a trip to the moon, the landscape in Iceland is what it must look like. I was there in November, so it was not sunny. By 4:00 p.m., the sun was gone. When we could see the outline of the sun, it seemed ethereal, not the big orange ball we are used to seeing in the Midwest.

Every stop we made on the Golden Circle was amazing. The geothermal landscape provides energy to the geysers and lagoons. The Blue Lagoon is a must-stop for every visitor. The outside temperature may be in the single digits, but that doesn't stop you from donning a swimsuit, walking outside, and jumping into the steam-heated lagoon. While enjoying the warm waters, you may be served champagne and can partake of a massage, if you desire.

Iceland is also noted for its small horses. They may be the height of a pony, but they are strong beyond their size. I had an opportunity to take a ride on one of the horses. They are quite furry, almost like a furry dog. That fur is good enough to keep the horses warm in the long winter months.

Visiting Iceland in November, I thought, would make

for a good opportunity to see the northern lights. But it was not to be. We searched every night, but the lights were just as elusive as the sun. There was a wonderful photo of the lights in full color, so I took a picture of the photo and told the people at home how lovely the northern lights could have been.

If you are a frequent flier or a timid traveler, put Iceland on your list of places to visit. You will not be disappointed. It is magic land and offers many opportunities to be amazed. The Viking museum on the island will answer many of the questions you may have. You realize how much the Vikings traveled and how much of their influence they left behind.

By the way, Iceland's neighboring island, Greenland, is not green. That's where the ice is stored, at least for now until climate change hits that island and erodes the landscape. I did not stop in Greenland, but it may be on my own must-see list.

SCANDINAVIA

The fjords of Scandinavia always held a special interest to me. In fact, the word *fjord*, first encountered in about fourth grade, was always intriguing to me. How many words do you know that start with "fj"? Scandinavia proved to be just as interesting and intriguing as the word *fjord*. The blue waters surrounded by the snow-covered mountains were a feast for one's eyes.

Before I could enjoy those blue waters, I had to make a flight connection in Newark. I boarded the plane in Indianapolis on a beautiful clear day, not a cloud in the sky. I certainly had no worries about making my connection in New Jersey. After loading and rolling out onto the tarmac, we waited to take off. But we didn't. We just sat there. I kept looking at my watch, seeing the minutes tick away. Why weren't we moving? Finally the pilot announced there was a situation in New Jersey and we would be delayed because of it.

After an agonizing wait of over an hour, we took off. We were finally in the sky heading eastward. We landed, and I went through another stomach-wrenching moment of waiting for passengers ahead of me to get up, get their luggage from the overheads, and slowly move toward the exit. I bounded off plane, looking for the Scandinavian Airline terminal, and raced toward it.

I rounded a corner of the crowded airport and saw an attendant with Scan Air on her uniform. I ran up to her, and she said my name. She had been looking for me. The flight attendant was just closing the door when I yelled, "I am coming." I was the last person on the plane, and one seat was left. Someone was already in my assigned seat, but I was so happy to be on board that I said I would be happy to sit anywhere.

As you travel, many things happen that are not on your agenda. You have to learn to roll with the punches and adapt. But sometimes it can become stress-filled.

I landed in Copenhagen and waited with the rest of the plane passengers for our luggage, except mine did not arrive. I could not believe it. After I had raced to get on the plane, apparently my luggage had not kept up. It was still back in Newark. My luggage was delivered the next day to my hotel, just one of the minor disasters when you travel.

When you travel alone, you join the rest of the tour in the originating city, either Rome, Paris, Dublin, and so forth. You never know who your roommate is going to be until you meet her in the chosen city. Consequently I have had some interesting roommates. In Copenhagen, I met the most delightful roommate possible. She was from Tasmania. She and her husband had left England fifty years ago and settled in Tasmania. We hit it off right away and had a great time with the rest of the group touring Denmark, Norway, and Sweden.

We happened to be in Scandinavia in mid-June, so we were lucky to be there for the summer solstice. It never got dark. At three o'clock in the morning, the sky still held some color. We had glorious sunshine the whole ten days we were there.

While in Denmark, I met the Little Mermaid and the queen. The queen was at her summer palace, and since we were in the neighborhood, our guide insisted we stop in her large courtyard to say hello. The queen accommodated us by coming to her front door and giving us a royal wave. We were told she was busy baking cookies. Who would have thought that a queen baked her own chocolate chip cookies? The amazing things you learn while traveling.

After leaving Denmark, we visited Norway. June weather could not have been nicer. I was told that the winters can be brutal, which bred a fierce tribe. You know them as Vikings. Norway at one time was the poor relative in Scandinavia, but when oil was discovered in the North Sea, it became one of the most prosperous countries.

Oslo was bathed in sunshine when we arrived on Sunday. Many of Oslo's citizens were enjoying the beautiful weather, and happy people filled the streets. Since it was a Sunday, I asked about churches. A Catholic church, I was told, was just a block away. It was a big brick building. "You can't miss it," they said.

I entered the big brick building and soon discovered a female preacher was starting the services speaking Norwegian. I realized I was in the wrong church, but I certainly was not going to leave. So I enjoyed my first Lutheran service. Another interesting part of traveling is doing something surprisingly different and accepting it as a learning experience.

The Nobel Peace Center, an impressive building, is in the middle of Oslo. Touring through Norway, we discovered the Norwegians have a quirky sense of humor and they love their trolls.

As we were leaving Norway, we stopped at the Olympic site of Lillehammer where the ski events were held. My roommate and I climbed to the top of the giant slope. There was no snow or skiers in June, but just the height of the slopes is enough to admire the Olympic skiers.

We crossed the border into Sweden as Stockholm was our destination. Stockholm stretches over fourteen islands. We toured the city with all of its historic sights and enjoyed the warmth of the city and its citizens. We did, however, find a very cold place, Stockholm's famous Ice Bar. With warm coats and mittens provided, our tour group raised our icy glasses to toast our trip and to say goodbye to Scandinavia.

Keep traveling!

LILLEHAMMER NORWAY

ANOTHER C IN MY LIFE

IMAGE PLASTIC MASK

I have been guided in life, especially in older years, by the three Cs: challenge, change, and choices. The older one gets, the more likely we will experience all of those. Many challenges crop up with the years. The challenges bring changes, and choices have to be made whether you want make them to or not.

The new C in my life was cancer. I never expected this

disease would happen to me. I am sure every cancer patient has expressed the same thought.

Several doctors confirmed that the small, inconspicuous growth on my neck was indeed cancerous, a dangerous kind of cancer called Merkel cell carcinoma. This type of cancer can spread quickly and quietly to lymph nodes. If you or a loved one has a suspicious growth that looks a little funny and will not go away, go to a medical facility and have it checked. No matter how small or inconspicuous it seems, you must seek attention.

I happened to mention to my cousin my strange little growth that would not heal. She strongly encouraged me to have the growth looked at just in case. I took her advice and made an appointment the next day.

After I published my first book, *Old Librarians Never Die, They Jump Out of Airplanes*, I gave many book presentations. I encouraged other women to meet the challenges of older years. Now it was my turn to meet a challenge. Let's see if I can challenge the big C. Let's see if I can adapt to the changes it will bring to my life. Let's see if I can make the correct changes.

I was introduced to more doctors in that two-month period than I had seen in my whole life. My personal doctor, after looking at the suspicious mole on my neck, sent me to a dermatologist. The dermatologist sent me to an oncologist, who sent me to the plastic surgeon in case I needed to cover the scar I would have on my neck after the operation.

Before the surgery, I had body scans from head to toe. With every scan, the various doctors found various maladies. First, it was my brain; something was not quite normal.

Moving down, my heart was not beating properly, something called a basil branch bundle. Another discovery was that my ovaries were not acting normal. In my eighth decade, I had to be concerned about my ovaries?

After worrying about all my abnormalities for a week, I finally received the results. Brain: normal. Heart: normal. Ovaries: questionable (worry about those later).

When the operation on my neck to remove the mole was completed, it was found that one of the lymph nodes did contain cancer. The doctor explained that other lymph nodes could be cancerous as well. I was given two choices: another operation to remove other nodes or radiation for six weeks. My choice was radiation for six long weeks.

On my first appointment with the radiologists, a mask made of white, porous plastic was formed of my face and shoulders. I was told I had to wear that mask every day I was zapped with radiation. What I was not told the first day was that while wearing the plastic mask, I would be bolted to a table, making it impossible for me to move, making sure the radiation would hit the target. While strapped to the table, my claustrophobia quickly kicked in.

The radiologists were understanding and tried to allay my fears of being strapped down and unable to move. But when they left the room and went to their shielded bunker, I wanted to yell, "'Where are you going?"

The thirty-three days of my radiation finally ended. I was presented a little stuffed bear, and the staff congratulated me for being a good patient. I, in turn, congratulated all medical people for helping me get through my adventure with cancer. So far it has been successful.

While masked and strapped to the table, I found a couple of ways to calm myself and stifle my claustrophobia. I said the Rosary on my fingers; nothing like a little help from above. My other amusement was to learn the alphabet backward. Just ask me: z, y, x, w, v, u, and so on.

I caution you again: if you have any mole or growth that looks unhealthy, please see your doctor. Sometimes it takes another person to push you out the door. I would not have sought help that quickly if not for my cousin motivating me to get the mole checked out. (Thanks, Verda.)

Recommended reading: *Cancer, Now What? Taking Action, Finding Hope, and Navigating the Journey Ahead* by Kenneth C. Hauck, PhD.

SENSE OF HUMOR

I was never considered smart or beautiful. What I was graced with was a sense of humor. I figured when I was born, God declared, "Give that girl a sense of humor. She's going to need it." A gift for which I am eternally grateful. In most situations in life, I have discovered that there is some element of humor involved—every situation except death, that is. There is nothing funny about death. It is so damn final—no reset button, no backspace, and no Esc button. The Delete button and End buttons would be more fitting.

Some days that humor element is harder to find. You may have to search for that bit of humor, but it is there. As a caregiver to my husband who was suffering from Parkinson's disease, there were many times when a sense of humor outranked my frustrations of caregiving. I had hidden his car keys before I had gone to work. So while I was ensconced in a feeling of safety for my husband at home, he was busy searching for and finding another set of car keys in the house. When I received a call at the library from the local hospital telling me my husband had been in an automobile wreck and was now a patient at the hospital, I was not in a laughing mood.

It seemed he had driven out to the McDonald's for a strawberry milkshake. His appetite apparently overruled his sense of propriety. On the drive home, with his coveted milkshake in hand, he somehow lost control of his car and hit a parked truck, bounced off a tree, and rolled into a person's screened-in porch. Fortunately little damage was done to the truck, tree, and porch.

However, when the ambulance was called, the EMTs were alarmed when they discovered the red liquid all over the inside of the car. Naturally, being medical people, they assumed it was blood and rushed him to the hospital. Do you see the humor in this? Thank you, God.

I dashed to the hospital, and the medical staff assured me, after checking him for several hours, he had no broken bones or any other medical malfeasance.

As I was rolling him out of the hospital in a wheelchair, a nurse rushed over and declared, "Stop. We didn't check his nose to see if it is broken."

I'm not a medical person, but what if it were broken? What can you do with a broken nose except let it heal? It was another hour of waiting. Finally he came again into the lobby, and the same nurse assured me that his nose was not broken and he could go home and heal. And I could go home and relax and wait for the next humorous episode.

The *Journal of Personality and Social Psychology* reported that women who had the biggest smiles in their high school / college yearbook photos had happier lives, happier marriages, and fewer personal setbacks in the next thirty years. Check your yearbook and mine.

"When you're smiling, the whole world smiles with you" should be your mantra. Smiling, it seems, engages at least three major muscle groups, increasing blood flow to the face and creating a rosy glow. Draw back your lips, and your raised cheeks round out your face, softening it. (So why won't the DMV people let you smile while taking your picture for your driver's license? Apparently they don't want you looking like a happy Hoosier driver, I guess.)

Anyway, put more smiles and laughter in your life. Walk through a shopping mall by yourself and keep smiling. You may be amazed how many people smile back.

Recommended reading: *Never Too Old to Laugh: A Laugh Out-Loud Collection of Cartoons, Quotes, Jokes and Trivia on Growing Older* by Ed Fischer.

CPSIA information can be obtained
at www.ICGtesting.com
Printed in the USA
BVHW032151261021
620002BV00004B/115

9 781663 213341